WESTCHESTER PUBLIC LIBRARY

7001 9100 584 467 0

D1543281

INSIDE LAW ENFORCEMENT

INSIDE THE FBI

Mythili Sampathkumar

Enslow Publishing
101 W. 23rd Street
Suite 240
New York, NY 10011
USA
enslow.com

Published in 2020 by Enslow Publishing, LLC
101 W. 23rd Street, Suite 240, New York, NY 10011

Copyright © 2020 by Enslow Publishing, LLC.

All rights reserved.

No part of this book may be reproduced by any means without the written permission of the publisher.

Library of Congress Cataloging-in-Publication Data

Names: Sampathkumar, Mythili, author.
Title: Inside the FBI / Mythili Sampathkumar.
Description: New York : Enslow Publishing, 2020 | Series: Inside law enforcement |
Audience: Grade level 5-8. | Includes bibliographical references and index.
Identifiers: LCCN 2018058102| ISBN 9781978507357 (library bound) | ISBN
9781978508552 (pbk.)
Subjects: LCSH: United States. Federal Bureau of Investigation—Juvenile literature. |
Confidential communications—United States—Juvenile literature.
Classification: LCC HV8141 .S286 2019 | DDC 363.250973—dc23
LC record available at https://lccn.loc.gov/2018058102

Printed in the United States of America

To Our Readers: We have done our best to make sure all website addresses in this book were active and appropriate when we went to press. However, the author and the publisher have no control over and assume no liability for the material available on those websites or on any websites they may link to. Any comments or suggestions can be sent by email to customerservice@enslow.com.

Photo Credits: Cover, p. 1 Marija Stojkovic/Shutterstock.com; p. 5 Ralf-Finn Hestoft/Corbis Historical/Getty Images; pp. 8, 11 Bettmann/Getty Images; p. 12 Jack Manning/Archive Photos/ Getty Images; p. 15 Jonathan Weiss/Shutterstock.com; pp. 16, 22, 25 © AP Images; p. 19 Shawn Thew/AFP/Getty Images; p. 28 Mark Wilson/Getty Images; p. 31 Splash News/Newscom; p. 32 Joe Raedle/Getty Images; p. 35 Pool/Getty Images; p. 37 Collection Christophel/Alamy Stock Photo; p. 38 Dean Drobot/Shutterstock.com.

CONTENTS

INTRODUCTION

One of the oldest federal agencies, the Federal Bureau of Investigation (FBI) has evolved over the last one hundred years to become the Department of Justice's main law enforcement agency. This book will explore the bureau's history, agents, law enforcement reach, and role as part of the American intelligence community, and the public storms weathered by the bureau.

The FBI's main mission is to protect and defend the United States and to enforce criminal laws of the country, particularly if crimes involve crossing state lines when state and local police do not have jurisdiction, or authority, to enforce laws. Founded in 1908 as the Bureau of Investigation, the agency has undergone numerous changes over time but has maintained its core purpose: to uphold the US Constitution.

The bureau's work ranges from protecting the country from terrorist attacks, foreign intelligence operations and spies, cyber attacks or hacking, and public corruption. The bureau employs around 35,000 people, including special agents, administrative support personnel, intelligence analysts, language experts, forensic scientists, and information technology specialists. By 2016, the FBI's budget was $8.7 billion[1], which included improving its cybersecurity operations, a growing part of the bureau.[2]

FBI director Christopher Wray was appointed by President Donald Trump and confirmed by Congress in August 2017. FBI directors are

The FBI is not only one of the oldest law enforcement agencies in the United States, but one of the most famous as well, having been around for more than 110 years.

limited to ten-year terms and preside over several deputy directors and eleven executive assistant directors for various sections of the bureau.

The FBI works around the world, but its headquarters are based in Washington, DC, at the J. Edgar Hoover Building. There are 56 field offices in all the major cities in the United States and 350 satellite offices in smaller cities and towns.[3] In addition, the bureau has a presence in 60 international offices. These are called legal attachés and are usually housed under the US embassy or consulate in that location.

Though the focus of the bureau is mostly domestic, the FBI can and does carry out some investigative and secret operations in other countries, but it requires coordination with headquarters and other government agencies.

Over the last several decades, the bureau has evolved from doing investigative work to being focused on crime prevention as well, especially concerning terrorism. It is part of the Joint Terrorism Task Force, a partnership between several federal, state, and local law enforcement agencies that investigate terrorism, wire fraud, and identity theft associated with terrorist activities.

The agency's motto is "Fidelity. Bravery. Integrity."[4] It can be traced back to a piece written by the editor of the agency's internal magazine, called *The Investigator.* W. H. Drane Lester wrote in September 1935:

> At last we have a name that lends itself to dignified abbreviation the Federal Bureau of Investigation, which quite naturally becomes "FBI." In the past our nicknames, which the public are so prone to give us, have been many and varied...the one which has become most widespread, is "G-Men," an abbreviation itself for "Government Men."
>
> But "F B I" is the best and one from which we might well choose our motto, for those initials also represent the three things for which the Bureau and its representatives always stand: "Fidelity - Bravery - Integrity."[5]

The FBI seal, also adopted in 1935, has special meaning as well. The blue background and scales depicted on the shield in the center of the seal represent justice. There are also thirteen stars circling the seal, which signify the original thirteen colonies that went on to become the United States, and there are two laurel branches—traditionally symbolizing academic achievement and distinction—with forty-six leaves in each because there were forty-six states when the FBI was established. The red and white stripes are, of course, borrowed from the American flag, while the "peaked bevelled edge which circumscribes the seal symbolizes the severe challenges confronting the FBI and the ruggedness of the organization. The gold color in the seal conveys its overall value."[6]

CHAPTER 1

A HISTORY OF THE FBI

The FBI as we know it was established in 1935, but there were a few early versions of it first. In the early 1900s, President Theodore Roosevelt was worried about anarchists, or those who believe governments are harmful and unnecessary to people. This worry was brought about after the assassination of President William McKinley in 1901 by anarchists.

At the time, the Department of Justice (DOJ) was already regulating interstate commerce, setting the rules for selling and buying goods across state lines. However, the agency had a staff shortage and was plagued by a large fraud scandal around that time that involved several federal government land grants being illegally obtained in Oregon with the help of members of Congress.

In the early days of the FBI, experts compared fingerprints manually, using only their eyes and a magnifying glass to match a suspect's prints to those found at the crime scene.

Fighting Corruption

In an attempt to fight that corruption and track and investigate suspected anarchists, Roosevelt gave the attorney general, the chief of the DOJ, authority to establish a law enforcement and investigative agency under the DOJ's authority. Then-Attorney General Charles J. Bonaparte hired thirty-four people, including some investigators from the Secret Service, which protects the US president, to begin the Bureau of Investigation on July 26, 1908.[1] This is why the FBI sits under the umbrella of the DOJ today.

This new agency's first director, known as the chief at that point, was Stanley Finch. One of the first tasks of this new agency was to enforce what was called the Mann Act, which made it a crime to transport or kidnap "any woman or girl for the purpose of prostitution or debauchery, or for any other immoral purpose" across state lines.

J. EDGAR HOOVER

J. Edgar Hoover was appointed in 1924 to the FBI's predecessor, the Bureau of Investigation, and then became the first director of the FBI as we know it in 1935. He was the longest-serving director in bureau history, leading the organization for thirty-seven years until his death in 1972. As a result, he shaped much of the bureau on the job since there was no precedent for much of the bureau's work or his position. Hoover became a powerful figure in Washington, DC, after collecting information in secret files on political leaders and civil rights activists like Malcolm X, Martin Luther King Jr., the Black Panther Party, and John Lennon of the Beatles in the 1950s and 1960s. Critics have said Hoover overstepped the boundaries of his authority, however, and used the FBI to threaten people he thought were radicals against the government, activists, and even politicians. President Harry S. Truman accused Hoover of forming his own "secret police" with his abuse of power.[2]

It was also known as the "White Slave Traffic Act" because investigators often arrested minorities or immigrant men seen with white women at the time. The act has since been revised to include more clear language, but it still prohibits sex trafficking.

Finally in 1935, after a few more name changes, the Federal Bureau of Investigation was established as an independent agency under the DOJ.

In the wake of World War I and the rise of Nazis in Europe, the FBI was given permission to monitor and investigate any people in the United States suspected of being affiliated with Nazis, and by 1939 Roosevelt had given his permission for the bureau to investigate espionage as well, while working with defense intelligence agencies.

World War II and the Growth of the FBI

J. Edgar Hoover is credited by some with making the FBI "into a modern, national organization stressing professionalism and scientific crime-fighting. Though he took on the role of director in 1924, when the agency was still known as the Bureau of Investigation, he was also instrumental in the founding of the FBI. In the 1930s, during the Great Depression, Hoover was responsible for taking down the country's most notorious gangsters, including bank robber John Dillinger and a kidnapper known as Machine Gun Kelly. In the 1940s, Hoover was responsible for directing the agency's wiretapping efforts—or eavesdropping via phone—targeted at people suspected of being Nazi sympathizers. For most of his life, Americans considered him a hero. He made the G-Man brand so popular that, at its height, it was harder to become an FBI agent than to be accepted into an Ivy League college."[3]

In the 1950s, the FBI, still under the direction of Hoover, began a program to crack down on organized crime. It was later aided by the Racketeer Influenced and Corrupt Organizations (RICO) Act[4] in 1970,

J. Edgar Hoover is known for modernizing the FBI and helping to track down some of America's most notorious criminals, such as John Dillinger and Machine Gun Kelly.

which allowed leaders of criminal organizations, like the heads of mafia families for example, to be tied to, and prosecuted for, crimes they ordered members of the organization to commit.

In May 1972, the agency began hiring female special agents, but it was still considered a difficult place to get hired as a woman or a minority. However, both groups have become a regular part of operations today. At least 13,000 FBI employees are women, with around 7,000 minorities and over 1,000 people with disabilities.[5]

Thanks to the RICO Act, the FBI had a much easier time bringing down organized crime bosses, including Carlo Gambino, pictured here at his arrest.

Special teams have been established through the decades for forensic analysis, like DNA testing at the FBI Laboratory[6], hostage negotiations, and special events coverage for Olympics held in the United States. The bureau increased its counterterrorism operations after the first World Trade Center bombing in New York City in 1993, and these operations continue today.

The FBI in the 21st Century

After the September 11, 2001, terrorist attacks, the FBI underwent a major change to streamline its operations and better handle potential threats. All terror-related operations were centralized, rather than being handled by the local FBI offices. The agency also divided operations into two separate branches, one focused on crime, and one on terrorism. This was done to allow each part of the bureau to get the resources and attention it needed, and to allow the agents in each division to focus fully on one particular area of investigation.

The FBI has also expanded its operations. Not only has it opened numerous overseas offices since 2001 and amped up its intelligence-gathering operations, but the FBI also shifted more attention to cybersecurity as the threat of computer-based attacks grew. It is no longer enough for the bureau to focus on the crimes happening physically within the borders of the United States. They now must police the internet and track down criminals attacking US citizens online, no matter where in the world they may be.

As the FBI has become more sophisticated, however, so have the criminals and terrorists. The FBI was unable to prevent the Fort Hood, Texas, mass shooting in 2009 or the Boston Marathon bombing in 2013. The bureau has also been criticized for its inability to prevent numerous school shootings, including the Parkland, Florida, attack in 2017, which left seventeen people dead.

CHAPTER 2

WHAT DOES THE FBI DO?

The six branches of the FBI plus the Office of the Director have a wide variety of responsibilities. While the FBI is not legally independent of the DOJ, it is "spiritually, culturally pretty independent"[1] and operates like its own federal agency, though subject to the authority of the attorney general.

The branches are specialized accordingly:

- Intelligence
- National Security
- Criminal, Cyber, Response, and Services Branch
- Information and Technology Branch
- Human Resources Branch

While the FBI is a well-known agency, most people don't realize that the agency is responsible for more than simply catching criminals and mobsters, though it does those things, too.

Offices that handle public affairs, coordinate with Congress, manage legal counsel, and perform certain administrative functions fall under the Office of the Director, headed by Christopher Wray beginnning in 2018.

Intelligence

The intelligence unit was formed in the wake of the terrorist attacks on September 11, 2001. The 9/11 Commission, which was set up to assess how the attacks were able to be carried out and how they could have

Like most federal law enforcement agencies in the 21st century, the FBI must be prepared to stop or prevent cyber or computer-based crimes, which are becoming more common every year.

been prevented, recommended to the FBI that it place a greater importance on the role intelligence—or information that could be crucial to making decisions—played in the bureau's work.

After a few different phases, the Intelligence Bureau began operating as an independent section of the FBI in 2014 under then director James Comey. This section is comprised of approximately seven thousand employees and makes the FBI an important part of the US intelligence community[2], a group of seventeen federal agencies.

The intelligence branch of the FBI is tasked with collecting information for the bureau. With approval from federal judges, agents use resources like wiretaps—electronic eavesdropping that allows an agent to listen to both sides of a phone call without either party knowing—to get information about people they believe are at risk of harming Americans.

National Security

The national security branch was established in 2005 after a need to combine the missions, resources, skills, and tasks of the FBI's counterterrorism and counterintelligence operations. The mission of this division's employees is to protect the United States from national security threats in all forms but particularly weapons of mass destruction, terrorism, and foreign espionage operations.

Like the intelligence branch, this branch also allows the FBI to play a critical role in the US intelligence community in sharing analysis of intelligence and information on possible threats with other agencies to collaborate and minimize them. Called a "domestic spy service"[3] by some, part of the authority of this division allows for agents to seize property of those suspected of working with weapons of mass destruction and helps lower barriers of communication and sharing between the Central Intelligence Agency (CIA) and the FBI. Both this and the intelligence branch have their own dedicated special agents.

Criminal, Cyber, Response, and Services

This is the largest branch within the FBI, and it was re-formed in 2002 as well. The division and its agents, analysts, and computer scientists have been tasked with the actual criminal investigative mandate of the FBI. This is also the branch that is required to protect the civil rights of people in the United States as well as investigate white collar, violent, and organized crimes; public corruption; and cyber-related crimes.

Corruption can include border corruption—drug trafficking, smuggling of illegal goods, or human trafficking—prison officials who take bribes or are exploited by prisoners, and election fraud, or it can include foreign entities and bribery. White collar crimes are usually financially motivated violations of the law done by professional or government officials and include fraud, money laundering, and even intellectual property theft, which is when people or companies are robbed of their ideas, inventions, and creative expressions.

In addition, the division operates the 24/7 cyber command center, called CyWatch. The center combines intelligence and abilities of the GBO, the National Cyber Investigative Joint Task Force. The center's larger purpose is to help in the event of a major cyber attack or hack on any critical informational technology infrastructure in the United States. If that happens, CyWatch can provide connectivity to other similar

BECOMING AN FBI SPECIAL AGENT

There are approximately 13,000 FBI special agents[4] employed by the bureau. To be a special agent you must be at least twenty-three years old and younger than thirty-seven years old; have at least a bachelor's degree, although further education like graduate and law degrees are looked at favorably; be physically fit; and be willing to sometimes put yourself in dangerous situations to protect people. The application process can take several months and involves interviews, written tests, lie detector or polygraph exams, a physical test—which involves a 300-meter run, one-minute of sit-ups, maximum number of push-ups, and a 1.5-mile run—drug tests, and a background check conducted by the bureau to determine a person's character, standing in the community, criminal and financial history, and medical history.

There are many special agents employed by the FBI, each of whom is well educated and physically fit, but many also have special skills, such as speaking a foreign language or knowing how to code.

federal agency cyber centers, government agencies, field office of the FBI, the legal attaches in embassies around the world, and some parts of the private sector if needed. This division also coordinates with other countries' FBI counterparts as well as Interpol.

Agents' Duties

In 2018, one of the priorities of the bureau was to recruit people with a background and interest in cybersecurity and degrees in computer science, computer forensics, engineering, and other technical fields that are in demand. People with foreign language skills are also sought after, particularly those who can speak Arabic, Farsi, Chinese, Korean, and Russian.

Agents have to obtain and maintain top security clearance in order to do their jobs, and they must spend twenty weeks at the FBI Academy in Quantico, Virginia[5], where they spend time in the classroom learning investigative and intelligence techniques, undergo physical fitness training, and learn the use of firearms. Only then can they become full agents.

FBI agents perform a variety of duties, including testifying in federal court, executing search warrants, making arrests, gathering evidence, interviewing sources, and fulfilling administrative duties. Some agents also work in specialized areas across the FBI, such as training, fingerprinting, lab services, and public affairs, while others serve as supervisors or managers. Agents do not have typical jobs and are often required to work long hours or could be transferred to other field offices depending on the needs of the bureau.

The bureau also employs people who do very normal jobs, like answer phones, manage the payroll, and fix the agency computers. Any job that is held in any other office exists in the FBI. In fact, much of the work done at the FBI would seem boring and ordinary—from cleaning the coffee makers to updating the computer software to making sure the lightbulbs in the overhead lights haven't burnt out. Many of these jobs, however, also require special security clearance. But these employees allow the agents to do their jobs and focus on catching terrorists and criminals without worrying that their computer will crash or their paycheck will be late.

CHAPTER 3

WHAT IS THE LEGAL AUTHORITY OF THE FBI?

The agency's authority to enforce laws is outlined in a regulation called Title 28 of the United States Code.[1] The regulation gives FBI agents the authority to make arrests for any federal crime suspected of being committed while they are present or when they have reasonable grounds to believe that person committed a felony, which is a serious crime often involving violence and usually carries a prison sentence of more than one year.

In general, the FBI can only make arrests while on US soil, but it has sometimes been given permission to make arrests outside the United States by foreign governments and Congress. When this happens, the same rules must be followed, and anyone arrested by an FBI agent must

The FBI is responsible for capturing people who have committed federal crimes, such as the woman here who tried to defraud Medicare, a national health care service, of $163 million.

be taken into FBI custody immediately and granted a trial as quickly as reasonably possible.

Corruption

The bureau also works to enforce two particular laws as well. The RICO Act, or the Racketeer Influenced and Corrupt Organizations Act, is the main tool the FBI uses to fight organized crime, crime that is committed by the mafia, gangs, and other groups, because it allows a leader of a group to be charged with the crime they ordered others in the group to carry out. Under RICO, a person committing "at least two acts of racketeering activity" from a list of twenty-seven federal and eight state crimes within ten years can be charged with racketeering—or repeated, continuous criminal operations. Usually it involves an illegal form of business or regularly taking money from people after threatening them, which is also called extortion. FBI investigators spend years building up cases against suspected criminals under this law. Some of the crimes included on the list include murder, kidnapping, robbery, bribery, fraud, copyright infringement, and terrorism.

The Patriot Act

The other law the FBI operates under is the USA Patriot Act, also known as the Uniting and Strengthening America by Providing Appropriate Tools Required to Intercept and Obstruct Terrorism Act of 2001.[2] The USA Patriot Act was signed into law by President George W. Bush in 2002. It was signed in the wake of the September 11 terrorist attacks, which killed nearly three thousand people from the United States and ninety different countries, injured more than six thousand, and prompted the country and the administration to take a hard look at the counterterrorism capabilities of law enforcement agents since the attackers had all been able to enter, live, and attend flight school in the United States.

The act essentially gave the FBI more license to wiretap people in the United States and monitor internet activity, a fact some critics said was overstepping the bureau's legal authority.[3] It also allowed the bureau to conduct what are called "sneak and peek"[4] operations with a warrant issued by a judge. This means they have the power to search a house while the residents are away but are not required to inform the residents for several weeks after the search.

While the FBI has jurisdiction, or legal authority, over a certain type of crime or geographic area that involves two or more states or territories, it is not a national police force.[5] State and local law enforcement agencies are not under the FBI's authority, though when it comes to complicated investigations the bureau sometimes takes the lead because it has better resources and technology than those smaller agencies.

The authority to arrest criminals in these instances depends on the crime police suspect the person committed.

Even though the FBI is the investigative wing of the DOJ, it does not actually take criminals to court itself. It conducts investigations and provides forensic analysis, and then submits that information to DOJ

INVESTIGATING CRIMES ON NATIVE AMERICAN RESERVATIONS

There are 565 federally recognized Native American tribes in the United States, and the FBI has law enforcement responsibility on 200 reservations, which are federal, protected lands. The FBI's jurisdiction over these areas is shared with the Bureau of Indian Affairs, which is part of the US Department of the Interior. More than one hundred agents in nineteen of the FBI's fifty-six field offices work on these matters full-time as part of the Indian Country Crimes Unit, investigating serious crimes such as murder, child or physical abuse, violent assault, drug trafficking, corruption, and Indian gaming law violations. There is also the Safe Trails Task Force, set up to help the FBI work with federal, state, local, and tribal law enforcement agencies in order to help keep crime down in Indian Country and allow for combining limited investigative and forensic resources to combat crime. The FBI's Office of Victim Assistance also has specialists dedicated to helping on Indian Country matters.[6]

While the FBI has a long and complicated history working with America's Native American population, it frequently steps in to help when crimes are committed on reservations in the United States.

lawyers who handle the prosecution of a criminal. Sometimes, however, FBI agents will be called to testify in court cases about the work they did on a particular investigation.

The FBI on Foreign Soil

While the Central Intelligence Agency, or CIA, is the primary American law enforcement agency operating outside of US borders, the FBI also works to protect American citizens overseas. Since the 1980s, the FBI has had jurisdiction in certain foreign investigations involving Americans. If an American citizen is the victim of a crime overseas, the US State Department will get permission from the country where the crime was committed for the FBI to operate within their borders to investigate the crime. Once the FBI is given permission to work in whatever country the crime was committed in, they can operate just as they would when investigating crimes in the US, and have the help of the local law enforcement agencies as well.

After a terror attack on the London subway in 2005, which injured not only English citizens, but Americans as well, the FBI worked with British authorities to investigate. The FBI also worked in Gaza in 2006 to help release a captured American reporter and cameraman.[7] Although the foreign authorities were involved in each case, the FBI takes their responsibility to protecting Americans seriously and does whatever they can to make sure US citizens receive justice no matter where they are when a crime is committed against them.

CHAPTER 4

CONTROVERSIES INVOLVING THE FBI

W hile Americans have long hailed the FBI as brave men and women fighting crime to protect innocent citizens, the bureau has come under fire for certain events in the past and has been rocked by an internal scandal.

In recent years, events across the country, as well as political battles in Washington, DC, have demanded that the bureau and its agents enforce certain laws or take certain actions even when they don't necessarily agree with the decision. Investigations into presidential candidate Hillary Clinton and her use of a personal email server caused some in the bureau

27

to question their work, while later investigations into President Trump were troubling for others in the agency.

Japanese Internment

In 1939 the bureau led the way in compiling lists of Japanese Americans who would be taken into internment camps in the United States. It was

Former FBI director James Comey investigated Hillary Clinton's private emails during the 2016 presidential election and then was fired by President Trump in 2017 while investigating him for collusion with Russia.

the beginning of World War II, and Japan was fighting against the United States, leading some in the government to fear that the Japanese would send spies to the US to attack. They began to suspect that the Japanese citizens who had immigrated to the US previously were potential terrorists. They even began to fear American-born Japanese people, believing that these citizens would be loyal to Japan and not the United States because of their heritage.

The FBI built the list from an existing one put together by US Navy intelligence, which had focused on Japanese Americans living on the West Coast or in Hawaii. The secret list contained the names of some German Americans and Italian Americans as well, because Germany and Italy were fighting on the same side as Japan. Together, the three countries were known as the Axis Powers, and the US feared that they would infiltrate US communities to bring the war to the American mainland.

Between 110,000 and 120,000 people of Japanese ancestry were held in internment camps despite the FBI actually concluding there was no

FORMER DIRECTOR JAMES COMEY

James Comey was the FBI director from 2013 to 2017, appointed by President Barack Obama and then fired by President Donald Trump. Comey's last year as FBI director, during the 2016 election, was plagued with controversy, beginning with his role in investigating presidential candidate Hillary Clinton and her use of a private email server to access her government emails when she was secretary of state under President Obama.[1] Comey also came under fire from Trump for not ending an investigation into whether there was collusion, or illegal collaboration, between the president's 2016 campaign team and officials from the Russian government.[2]

threat.[3] Public opinion had turned against the Japanese Americans, with several people questioning their loyalty to the United States as World War II raged on. The FBI was then tasked with protecting Japanese Americans once they were allowed to return to their homes after the war ended.

Celebrities Under Investigation

The FBI, as a result of its first director J. Edgar Hoover's habit of collecting information on US citizens he considered "subversive,"[4] has maintained files on a number of famous people either for opposing the Vietnam War, or because those people had been threatened or extorted for money at some point. Singers Michael Jackson, Bob Dylan, Frank Sinatra, and John Lennon, and actress Jane Fonda are just some of the people in FBI files.

A Spy Among Them

On February 20, 2001, the FBI announced it had arrested one of its own agents, Robert Hanssen, for being a spy. He had been a special agent with the bureau since 1976. Hanssen was involved in what was "possibly the worst intelligence disaster in US history."[5] He was ultimately convicted of selling US secrets to the Soviet Union, the communist authority that ruled over what is now Russia and several countries in Eastern Europe and northern and central Asia. It was also called the Union of Soviet Socialist Republics, or the USSR.

Hanssen gave confidential information to the USSR about what the United States would do in a nuclear war, the development of military weapons technology, America's counterintelligence program, and any Soviet spies who had betrayed the USSR to the CIA, among other things. This took place over the course of twenty-two years without anyone in the FBI finding out.

9/25/97

CLASSIFIED BY SSA 5668&D/JS
DECLASSIFY ON: 25X CA # 83-1720
3/25/97 39677SAH/JS
CLASSIFIED DECISIONS FINALIZED
BY DEPARTMENT REVIEW COMMITTEE (DRC)
DATE 2/12/86

~~SECRET~~

CONFIDENTIAL

April 25, 1972

BY LIAISON

1 - Mr. A. Rosen
1 - Mr. T. E. Bishop
1 - Mr. E. S. Miller
1 - Mr. R. L. Shackelford
1 - Mr. T. J. Smith (Horner)
1 - Mr. R. L. Pence

Honorable H. R. Haldeman
Assistant to the President
The White House
Washington, D. C. CA# 83-1720
CLASSIFIED DECISIONS FINALIZED
BY DEPARTMENT REVIEW COMMITTEE (DRC)
DATE 12/10/99 53A5668560/JS

Dear Mr. Haldeman:

John Winston Lennon is a British citizen and former
member of The Beatles singing group. ████████ Lennon has taken an interest in "extreme
left-wing activities in Britain" and is known to be a
sympathizer of Trotskyist communists in England.

Despite his apparent ineligibility for a United States
visa due to a conviction in London in 1968 for possession of
dangerous drugs, Lennon obtained a visa and entered the United
States in 1971. During February, 1972, a confidential source,
who has furnished reliable information in the past, advised that
Lennon had contributed $75,000 to a newly organized New Left
group formed to disrupt the Republican National Convention.
The visas of Lennon and his wife, Yoko Ono, expired on
February 29, 1972, and since that time Immigration and
Naturalization Service (INS) has been attempting to deport
them. During the Lennons' most recent deportation hearing at
INS, New York, New York, on April 18, 1972, their attorney
stated that Lennon felt he was being deported due to his
outspoken remarks concerning United States policy in Southeast
Asia. The attorney requested a delay in order that character
witnesses could testify for Lennon, and he then read into the
court record that Lennon had been appointed to the President's
Council for Drug Abuse (National Commission on Marijuana and
Drug Abuse) and to the faculty of New York University,
New York, New York.

Tolson
Felt
Campbell
Rosen
Mohr
Bishop
Miller, E.S.
Callahan
Casper

KDP:plm
(8)
100-469910

REC-105

~~SECRET~~ CONFIDENTIAL

Group 1

100-469910-7

19 APR 26 1972

SEE NOTE PAGE TWO

The FBI keeps files on everyone it investigates, including celebrities. Shown here is a
page from the files kept on musician John Lennon during the 1960s and 1970s.

CLASSIFIED BY: 25X 3.3 (6) 11/29/203/
DECLASSIFY ON:

Students mourn the loss of friends and classmates at a memorial for the seventeen murder victims of the Parkland, Florida, school shooting in 2018. Prior to the shooting, the FBI had received tips on the shooter.

When the Soviet Union collapsed in 1991, Hanssen then began secretly dealing with Russian intelligence and was doing so until his arrest in Vienna, Virginia, after an internal investigation that took several years and was sparked because of a tip from Hanssen's brother-in-law, who was also an FBI employee. He remained anonymous to Soviet and Russian intelligence officials, who paid him $1.4 million and gave him diamonds.

The Parkland Shooting

On February 14, 2018, a gunman shot and killed seventeen people, the majority of whom were students, at Marjory Stoneman Douglas High School in Parkland, Florida. The suspect, Nikolas Cruz, had been a student at the school. The FBI has been criticized[6] for not acting on two tips on Cruz provided to it anonymously through its Public Access Line, one in September 2017 and the other just one month prior to the shooting.

The first tip came after Cruz had posted a YouTube comment about wanting to become a school shooter. The tip was directed to an agent in Jackson, Mississippi, about 900 miles (1,448 kilometers) away from Parkland, Florida. The agent investigated the matter but was unable to identify Cruz, who had posted under an anonymous account. The agent never asked YouTube for the original posting nor to preserve the post. The matter was closed because it was not deemed a national security threat. The January 2018 tipster expressed concerns about Cruz's behavior and indicated the suspect was in possession of several guns.

The bureau said in a statement two days after the massacre, "The caller provided information about Cruz's gun ownership, desire to kill people, erratic behavior, and disturbing social media posts, as well as the potential of him conducting a school shooting."[7] After an internal investigation, the bureau said proper protocol had not been followed since the tip was never forwarded to the closest field office in Miami, Florida, and was thus never acted upon.

CHAPTER 5

THE FUTURE OF THE FBI

The future of the bureau will be determined by a number of factors, including who is in charge of the executive branch at any particular point, as well as what law enforcement issues the country is facing. The bureau is a product of the government that runs it, and any future it has will change as the politics surrounding its work change.

Since its beginning, the bureau has grown from thirty-four employees focusing on a limited set of interstate crimes to over 30,000 people focused on everything from investigating suspected anarchists, kidnapping, organized crime, financial white collar crime, counterterrorism, and computer systems hacking.

Changes in focus are inevitable, and the bureau is "always evolving to meet the threats of the moment. Each historic period has prepared us for the challenges of the future. And while it is a time of tremendous change in the Bureau, our values will not change."[1] The bureau has gone from

After James Comey (*right*) was fired by President Trump, experts suggested that the previously independent law enforcement agency would become more influenced by politics.

only investigating crimes to also becoming part of the US government's host of agencies focusing on national security and preventing terrorist attacks. Priorities could change to include more cybersecurity crimes in the near future. But the focus should always be on rule of law, upholding the US Constitution, and protecting civil liberties and rights.

The Political Future of the FBI

After President Donald Trump fired James Comey in May 2017, several experts predicted the future of the FBI will be more influenced by politics[2] than it has ever been before because many of the president's associates are under investigation and because of the controversial appointment of Supreme Court justice Brett Kavanaugh in 2018.

Kavanaugh was going through the Senate confirmation process to be named as one of the nine Supreme Court justices when a woman named Christine Blasey Ford came forward to accuse him of sexually assaulting her when they were both in high school in the 1980s. The accusations sparked heated debate all over the country and between Democrats, Republicans, and the president. Several people had called for the FBI to investigate the matter, while others felt the incident was too long ago to have any bearing on how Kavanaugh would do as a judge in the highest court in the country.

More and more young people have weighed in on what they think the bureau should be doing as well, something most Americans had likely never thought about before. In a poll, 80 percent of people thought the

THE FBI IN POP CULTURE

The FBI has fascinated crime novelists and movie directors for decades. Several television shows have been centered around the bureau, like the thriller *Quantico*, starring Priyanka Chopra, and *Bones*, about a forensic anthropologist who collaborates with the FBI to solve unusual crimes. Others include *Criminal Minds*, *White Collar*, and *The X-Files*, all focusing on special units within the bureau whose duties range from catching serial killers, art theft, and white collar crime, to investigating paranormal and extraterrestrial crimes. Some of the portrayals are accurate or perhaps based, in part, on actual events, and some are just fiction. According to the bureau, anyone wanting to write about the FBI can consult with it about "closed cases or our operations, services, or history. However, there is no requirement that they do so, and the FBI does not edit or approve their work."[3]

The FBI has been the basis for countless movies, books, and TV shows, including *Criminal Minds* (*above*), about a team of agents who profile serial criminals.

bureau should have investigated Ford's allegations.[4] The results of the poll could point to a future for the bureau that involves more politically motivated work, as guided by the country's leaders.

Tech and the FBI

As technology changes, so too will the bureau. Forensics experts are constantly fine-tuning ways to collect and analyze DNA, fingerprints, and other crime scene evidence. Databases of criminal activity and past criminals are growing more robust and are connected to various law enforcement agencies to make it easier and quicker to collaborate, share

As the FBI evolves in the coming years, it will likely add more cybersecurity roles, like hackers and computer experts, to its forces, requiring hopeful agents to acquire a whole new set of skills.

information, and tackle cases from a variety of perspectives. Cybersecurity is a field that has to constantly be on the lookout for new ways to protect computer systems, prevent new viruses that are developed to inflict damage, and track down hackers.

The face of the bureau will likely grow more diverse too as focus has moved toward recruiting more people with backgrounds in hard sciences, computer science, engineering, cybersecurity, and information technology, which are all linked to national security.

As the country and the world change, the FBI's makeup will also change. There will be more immigrants and people with diverse backgrounds joining the bureau, and the number of agents who speak foreign languages will likely also increase. The bureau will likely also face numerous new controversies in the coming years, due to the nature of the political landscape and the changing needs of America's law enforcement community. Whether the bureau weathers all these changes will depend on the people within the agency as well as those in government who work to support it.

CHAPTER NOTES

Introduction

1. Federal Bureau of Investigation, "FY 2017 Budget Request At A Glance," Justice.gov, https://www.justice.gov/jmd/file/822286/download.
2. Dustin Volz, "U.S. Spending Bill to Provide $380 Million to Election Cyber Security," Reuters, March 21, 2018, https://www.reuters.com/article/us-usa-fiscal-congress-cyber/u-s-spending-bill-to-provide-380-million-for-election-cyber-security-idUSKBN1GX2LC.
3. "Federal Bureau of Investigation: Our Locations," FBI.gov, https://www.fbi.gov/about/mission.
4. "Federal Bureau of Investigation: Our Motto," FBI.gov, https://www.fbi.gov/about/mission.
5. "Federal Bureau of Investigation: Seal & Motto," FBI.gov, https://www.fbi.gov/history/seal-motto.
6. Ibid.

Chapter 1: A History of the FBI

1. "Federal Bureau of Investigation: A Brief History," Fbi.gov, https://www.fbi.gov/history/brief-history.
2. Anthony Summers, "The Secret Life of J. Edgar Hoover," *The Guardian,* December 31, 2011, https://www.theguardian.com/film/2012/jan/01/j-edgar-hoover-secret-fbi.
3. Kenneth D. Ackerman, "Five Myths About J. Edgar Hoover," *Washington Post,* November 9, 2011, https://www.washingtonpost.com/opinions/five-myths-about-j-edgar-hoover/2011/11/07/gIQASLIo5M_story.html?utm_term=.f9998d8696c2.

4. "Racketeer Influenced and Corrupt Organizations (RICO) Law," Justia. com., https://www.justia.com/criminal/docs/rico/.
5. Ed Grabionowski, "How the FBI Works," HowStuffWorks, https:// people.howstuffworks.com/fbi.htm.
6. "Federal Bureau of Investigation: Laboratory Services," FBI.gov, https:// www.fbi.gov/services/laboratory.

Chapter 2: What Does the FBI Do?

1. Michael Schmidt and Matt Apuzzo, "Comey Told Sessions: Don't Leave Me Alone with Trump," *New York Times,* June 6, 2017, https://www. nytimes.com/2017/06/06/us/politics/comey-sessions-trump.html.
2. Zachary Laub, "FBI's Role in National Security," Council on Foreign Relations, June 21, 2017, https://www.cfr.org/backgrounder/fbis-role-national-security.
3. "Bush Sets up Domestic Spy Service," BBC News, June 30, 2005, http://news.bbc.co.uk/2/hi/americas/4636117.stm.
4. "Number of Federal Bureau of Investigation Employees in 2017, by Role and Gender," Statista.com, https://www.statista.com/statistics/745497/number-of-fbi-employees-by-gender/.
5. "FAQs: What kind of training does an agent go through?," Fbi.gov, https://www.fbi.gov/about/faqs/what-kind-of-training-does-an-agent-go-through.

Chapter 3: What Is the Legal Authority of the FBI?

1. "28 USC 33 - Federal Bureau of Investigation" United States Code, Gpo.gov, https://www.gpo.gov/fdsys/granule/USCODE-2010-title28/USCODE-2010-title28-partII-chap33.

2. "Uniting and Strengthening America by Providing Appropriate Tools Required to Intercept and Obstruct Terrorism Act of 2001," Public Law, 107th Congress. Gpo.gov, https://www.gpo.gov/fdsys/pkg/PLAW-107publ56/html/PLAW-107publ56.htm.

3. Spencer Ackerman, "FBI Used Patriot Act to Obtain 'Large Collections' of Americans' Data, DOJ finds," *The Guardian,* May 21, 2015, https://www.theguardian.com/us-news/2015/may/21/fbi-patriot-act-doj-report.

4. "How the USA Patriot Act Expands Law Enforcement 'Sneak and Peek' Warrants," ACLU.org, https://www.aclu.org/other/how-usa-patriot-act-expands-law-enforcement-sneak-and-peek-warrants.

5. Ed Grabionowski, "How the FBI Works," HowStuffWorks, https://people.howstuffworks.com/fbi.htm.

6. "Indian Country Crime." FBI.gov, https://www.fbi.gov/investigate/violent-crime/indian-country-crime.

7. "Protecting Americans Overseas," FBI.gov, https://archives.fbi.gov/archives/news/stories/2008/june/international_060308.

Chapter 4: Controversies Involving the FBI

1. Sean McElwee, Matt McDermott, and Will Jordan, "4 Pieces of Evidence Showing FBI Director James Comey Cost Clinton the Election," *Vox,* January 11, 2017, https://www.vox.com/the-big-idea/2017/1/11/14215930/comey-email-election-clinton-campaign.

2. Nate Silver, "The Comey Letter Probably Cost Clinton the Election," FiveThirtyEight, May 3, 2017, https://fivethirtyeight.com/features/the-comey-letter-probably-cost-clinton-the-election/.

3. ABC News, "Full James Comey Testimony on President Donald Trump, Russia Investigation at Senate Hearing," YouTube.com, https://www.youtube.com/watch?v=7j0f6c-3x6s.

4. JPat Brown, B. C. D. Lipton, and Michael Morisy, *Writers Under Surveillance: The FBI Files* (Cambridge, MA: MIT Press), 2018.

5. "Toyasaburo Korematsu v. United States (December 18, 1944)," FindLaw, https://caselaw.findlaw.com/us-supreme-court/323/214.html.

6. "A Review of FBI Security Programs, March 2002," Department of Justice, Commission for Review of FBI Security Programs, DOJ.gov, https://www.scribd.com/document/5362670/ashcroft-fbi.

7. Paula McMahon and Brittany Wallman, "How the FBI Botched Tips About the Parkland School Shooter," *South Florida Sun-Sentinel,* August 29, 2018, https://www.sun-sentinel.com/local/broward/parkland/florida-school-shooting/fl-florida-school-shooting-fbi-tips-problems-20180828-story.html.

Chapter 5: The Future of the FBI

1. "FBI Director James Mueller Statement Before the Senate Judiciary Committee," September 17, 2008, FBI.gov, https://archives.fbi.gov/archives/news/testimony/preparing-for-the-challenges-of-the-future.

2. Doug Wyllie, "3 Predictions on the Future of the FBI After Comey's firing," Police One, May 10, 2017, https://www.policeone.com/chiefs-sheriffs/articles/339368006-3-predictions-on-the-future-of-the-FBI-after-Comeys-firing/.

3. "How accurately is the FBI portrayed in books, television shows, and motion pictures?" FBI.gov, https://www.fbi.gov/about/faqs/how-accurately-is-the-fbi-portrayed-in-books-television-shows-and-motion-pictures.

4. "NowThis America's Future Poll: Nearly 80% of Young Adults Think FBI Should Investigate Allegations Against Supreme Court Nominee Brett Kavanaugh," NowThis/Group Nine Media, September 24, 2018, https://www.groupninemedia.com/press/nowthis-americas-future-poll-nearly-80-of-young-adults-think-fbi-should-investigate.

GLOSSARY

civil rights The rights of citizens to freedom and equality.

collusion Illegal, secret cooperation or conspiracy with an opposing group, particularly in order to cheat or deceive authorities or the public.

counterterrorism Political or military activities designed to prevent or thwart terrorism or terrorist activity.

cyber crime A criminal act done through the use of computers and/or the internet; often more generally called hacking.

cybersecurity The protection of any computer, hardware, or software systems connected to the internet from hackers or unauthorized intrusions.

espionage The act of spying or of using spies, usually by governments, to obtain political and military information about criminal groups or foreign countries.

felony A serious crime often involving violence that usually carries a prison sentence of more than one year.

forensics Scientific tests and procedures, like DNA testing and bullet, fingerprint, and/or computer systems analysis, done to help solve crimes.

fraud An act committed for illegal financial gain; a person who commits that crime.

human trafficking Like modern slavery, human trafficking involves trading people for forced labor or exploitation.

jurisdiction The official power to make legal decisions and judgments; the geographic area of authority.

organized crime Collective description of illegal activities that are planned, controlled, and carried out by powerful groups that consider themselves a gang, family, or other type of coordinated group.

racketeering The continuous act of getting involved in a dishonest and fraudulent business dealing or offering a service to solve a problem that wouldn't otherwise exist.

rule of law The principle that everyone is subject to a set of laws fairly applied and enforced.

white collar crime Crime that is financially motivated and nonviolent, committed by business or government professionals.

FURTHER READING

Books

Douglas, John, and Mark Olshaker. *Mindhunter: Inside the FBI's Elite Serial Crime Unit*. New York, NY: Gallery Books, 2017.

Elnoury, Tamer, and Kevin Maurer. *American Radical: Inside the World of an Undercover Muslim FBI Agent*. New York, NY: Dutton, 2017.

Grann, David. *Killers of the Flower Moon: The Osage Murders and the Birth of the FBI*. New York, NY: Doubleday, 2016.

Jamali, Naveed, and Ellis Henican. *How to Catch a Russian Spy: The True Story of American Civilian Turned Double Agent*. New York, NY: Scribner, 2015.

McGowan, Michael R., and Ralph Pezzulo. *Ghost: My Thirty Years as an FBI Undercover Agent*. New York, NY: St. Martin's Press, 2018.

Websites

Forensic Magazine
www.forensicmag.com
This online and print magazine focuses on the latest news about forensic science technology, trends, equipment, services, and lab design.

Investopedia
www.investopedia.com/terms/w/white-collar-crime.asp
Investopedia is an online financial news outlet. Its White Collar Crime page focuses specifically on information about white collar crimes being investigated by the FBI.

Justia
www.Justia.com
Justia provides free information on laws, regulations, and cases for students and professionals.